Unit 1

Yes/No* questions with *it's

Question				Answer		
Is	**it**	an	eraser?	Yes, **it is.**	**It's** an eraser.	*It's = It is*
		a	pen?	No, **it isn't.**	**It's** a crayon.	*isn't = is not*

***Is it** a clock? No, **it isn't**. **It's** a map.*

1 **Unscramble.** Write a question.

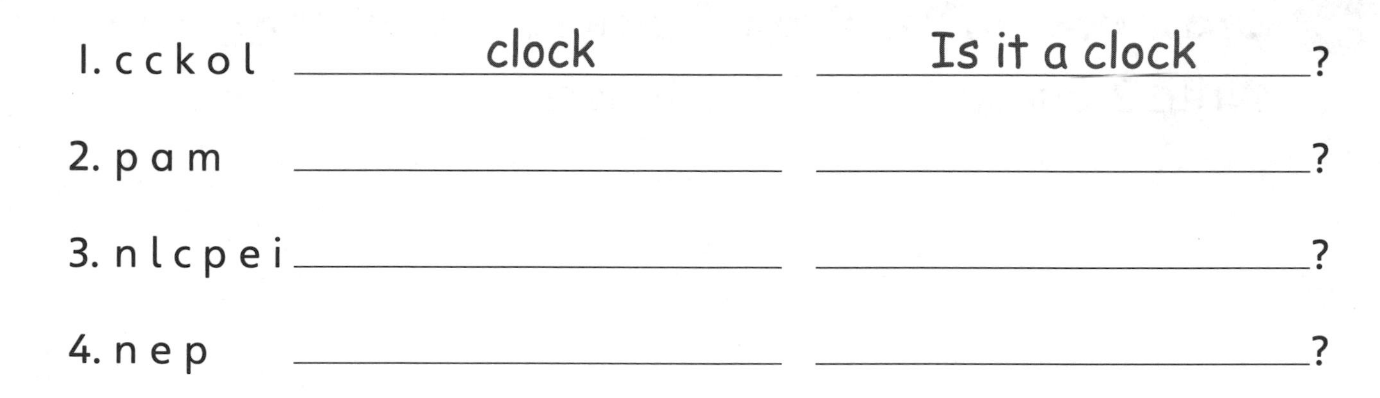

1. c c k o l ______clock______ ______Is it a clock______?
2. p a m ____________ ____________?
3. n l c p e i ____________ ____________?
4. n e p ____________ ____________?

2 **Look and read.** Write the answer.

1. Is it a clock? ______Yes, it is______.
2. Is it a crayon? ____________.
3. Is it a map? ____________.
4. Is it a chair? ____________.

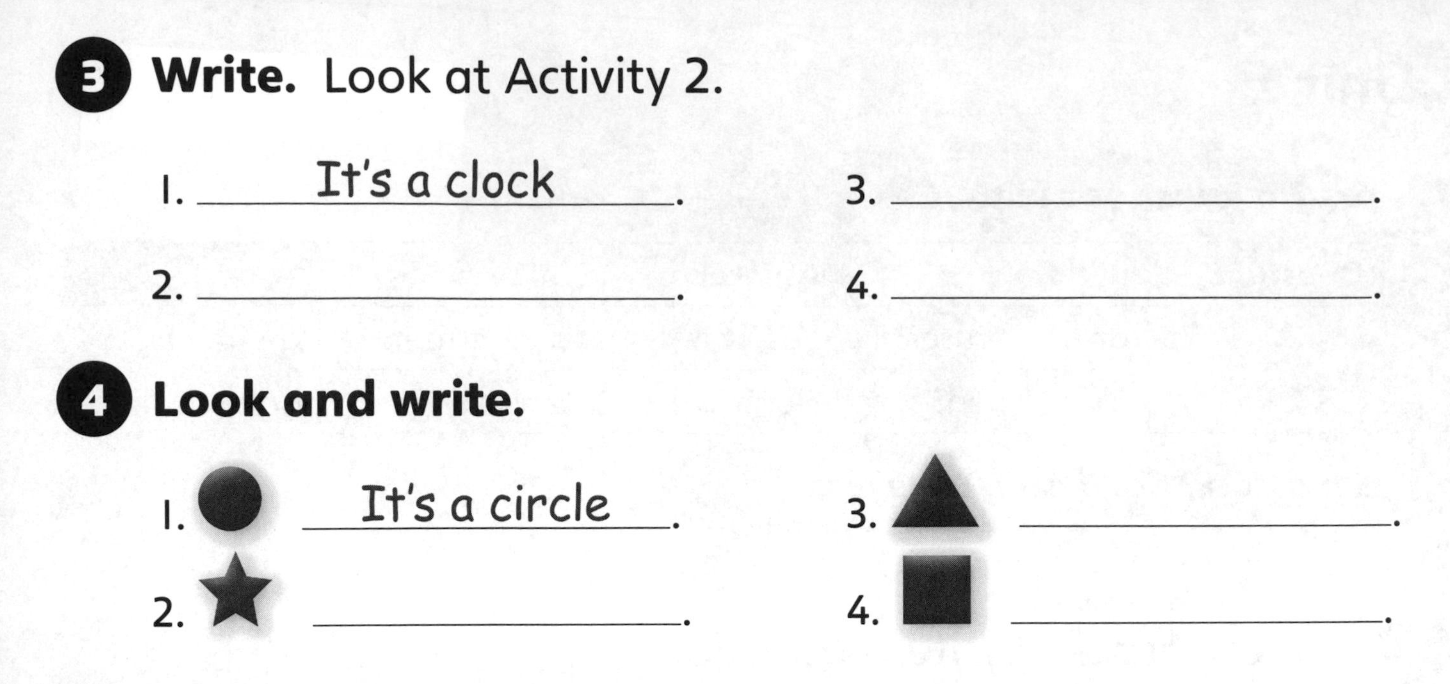

3 Write. Look at Activity 2.

1. It's a clock________.
2. ________________.
3. ________________.
4. ________________.

4 Look and write.

1. It's a circle________.
2. ________________.
3. ________________.
4. ________________.

5 Draw and write. Draw a picture of your classroom. Write 2 questions and 2 answers.

____

____

____

____

What and _How many_

Question				Answer
What		is	it?	It's an eraser.
	color	is	it?	It's orange.

Question	Answer
How many erasers?	Three.

What asks about a thing. *How many* asks for a number.

1 **Read and match.** Draw a line.

1. Is it a	a. it?
2. It's an	b. picture?
3. What color	c. is it?
4. What is	d. papers?
5. How many	e. eraser.

2 **Read.** Write *What*, *What's*, or *How*.

1. ______________ your name? I'm Sandy.
2. ______________ color is it? It's purple.
3. ______________ many pictures? Six.
4. ______________ is it? It's a chair.

3 **Read and write.** Complete the questions.

1. ______What is it______? It's a book.
2. ______________________? It's black.
3. ______________________ chairs? Five.

4 Look and write.

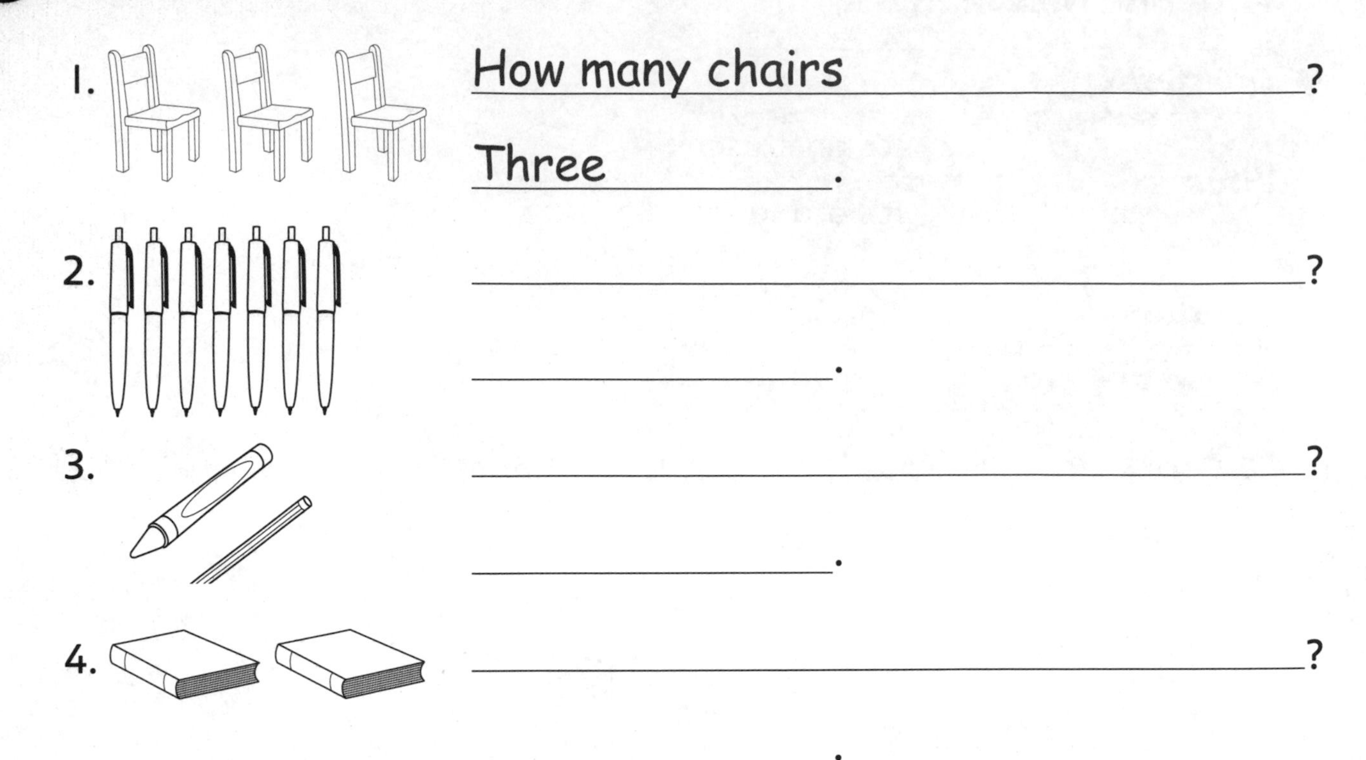

1. How many chairs ______?
   Three ______.
2. ______?
   ______.
3. ______?
   ______.
4. ______?
   ______.

5 **Write.** Color the picture. Answer the questions.

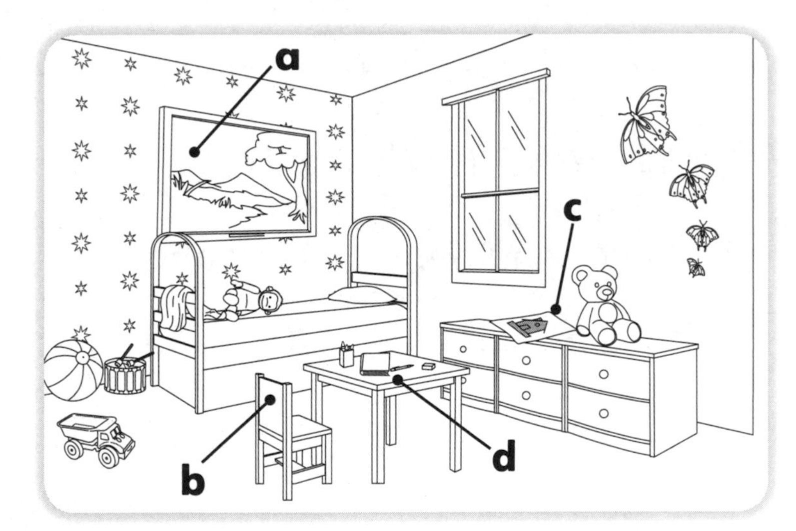

1. Look at **a**. What is it?
   ______.
2. Look at **b**. What color is it?
   ______.
3. Look at **c**. What is it?
   ______.
4. Look at **d**. What color is it?
   ______.

Unit 2

to be: is, are

Question			Answer		
What	**is**	it?	**It's**	a tree.	*It's = It is*
	are	they?	**They're**	trees.	*They're = They are*

one thing = ***It's*** *a bird*.

two or more things = ***They're*** *birds*.

1 Read. Circle the words.

1. **What** / **Is** it a river? Yes, it **is** / **are**.
2. What **is** / **are** it? It **'s** / **are** a butterfly.
3. What **is** / **are** they? They **is** / **are** trees.
4. **What** / **How** are they? **It's** / **They're** rocks.

2 Read. Rewrite the sentences.

1. It is a butterfly. It's a butterfly ______.
2. They are rocks. ______.
3. It is a bird. ______.
4. They are trees. ______.

3 **Look.** Write questions.

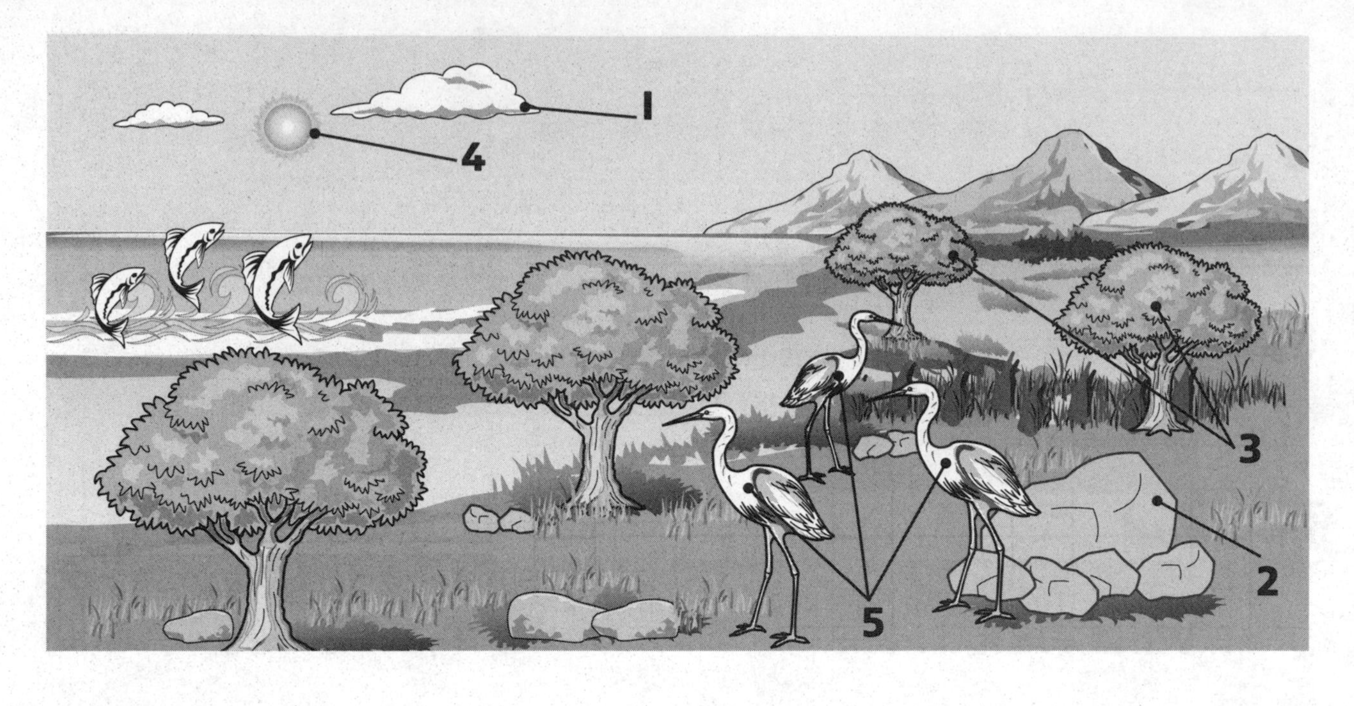

1. What is it?
2. ______________________?
3. ______________________?
4. ______________________?
5. ______________________?

4 **Look.** Answer the questions in Activity 3. Use the picture.

1. It's a cloud.
2. ______________________.
3. ______________________.
4. ______________________.
5. ______________________.

5 **Look and write.** Write 2 questions and 2 answers about the picture in Activity 2.

______________________? ______________________?

______________________. ______________________.

Where and *in* or *on*

Question			Answer
Where	is	the moon?	It's **in** the sky.
	are	the birds?	They're **on** the rock.

Use *in* or *on* + a place: ***in*** the tree, ***on*** the bush

1 **Read.** Circle the letter.

1. The clouds are ________ the sky. a. is b. on c. in
2. The rocks ________ in the river. a. is b. are c. on
3. The moon ________ in the sky. a. is b. on c. are
4. Where ________ the birds? a. is b. in c. are
5. The monkey is ________ the rock. a. in b. are c. on

2 **Look.** Write *in* or *on*.

1. The bird is _____ the tree.
2. The rocks are _____ the river.
3. The star is _____ the sky.
4. The bird is _____ the stick.

 **Look and write.**

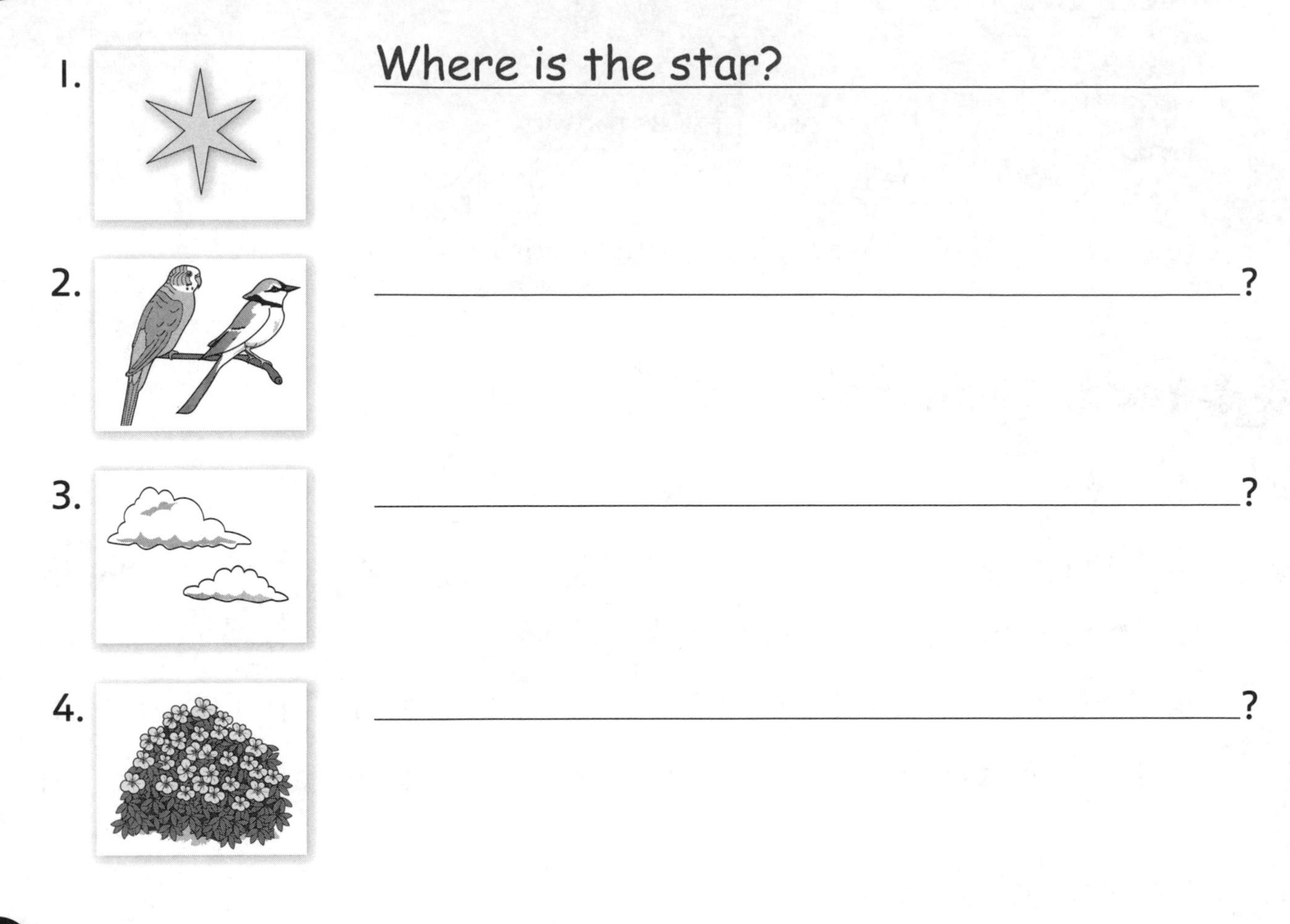

1. Where is the star?
2. ______________________?
3. ______________________?
4. ______________________?

4 Write. Answer the questions in Activity 3.

1. It's in the sky.
2. ______________.
3. ______________.
4. ______________.

 **Look and write.** Look outside. Write 3 questions and answers about what you see.

Where's the sun? It's in the sky.

____

____

____

Unit 3

to have

Question	Answer			
How many sisters do you have?	I	**have**	one sister.	*don't = do not*
		don't have	any sisters.	

*I **have** one sister/two brothers.*

*I **don't have** any brothers.*

1 **Write.** Unscramble the sentences.

1. brother / have / a / I / big

   I have a big brother.

2. have / sister / a / I

   ______.

3. a / don't / brother / I / have

   ______.

4. parents / I / two / have

   ______.

2 **Read and write.** Give answers that are true for you.

1. Do you have any sisters?

   ______.

2. How many parents ______?

   ______.

3. How many grandfathers ______?

   ______.

4. ______ any brothers?

   ______.

3 Look and write.

1. sister I don't have any sisters.
2. mother ______________________.
3. father ______________________.
4. brother ______________________.
5. grandfather ______________________.

4 **Write.** Write questions to ask a friend about family. Use the words in the box.

brother sister grandfather grandmother

1. Do you have a sister?
2. ______________________?
3. ______________________?
4. ______________________?

5 **Write.** Write 2 sentences about your family. Use *have*.

____

____

He/She and questions with *who*

Question		Answer	*Who's = Who is*
Who's	**he**?	**He's** my brother Jack.	*He's = He is*
	she?	**She's** my sister Ana.	*She's = She is*

Who asks about a person.

he = a boy/man *she* = a girl/woman

Look and write.

1. Who's he? 2. ____________ 3. ____________

Look and write. Imagine this is your family.

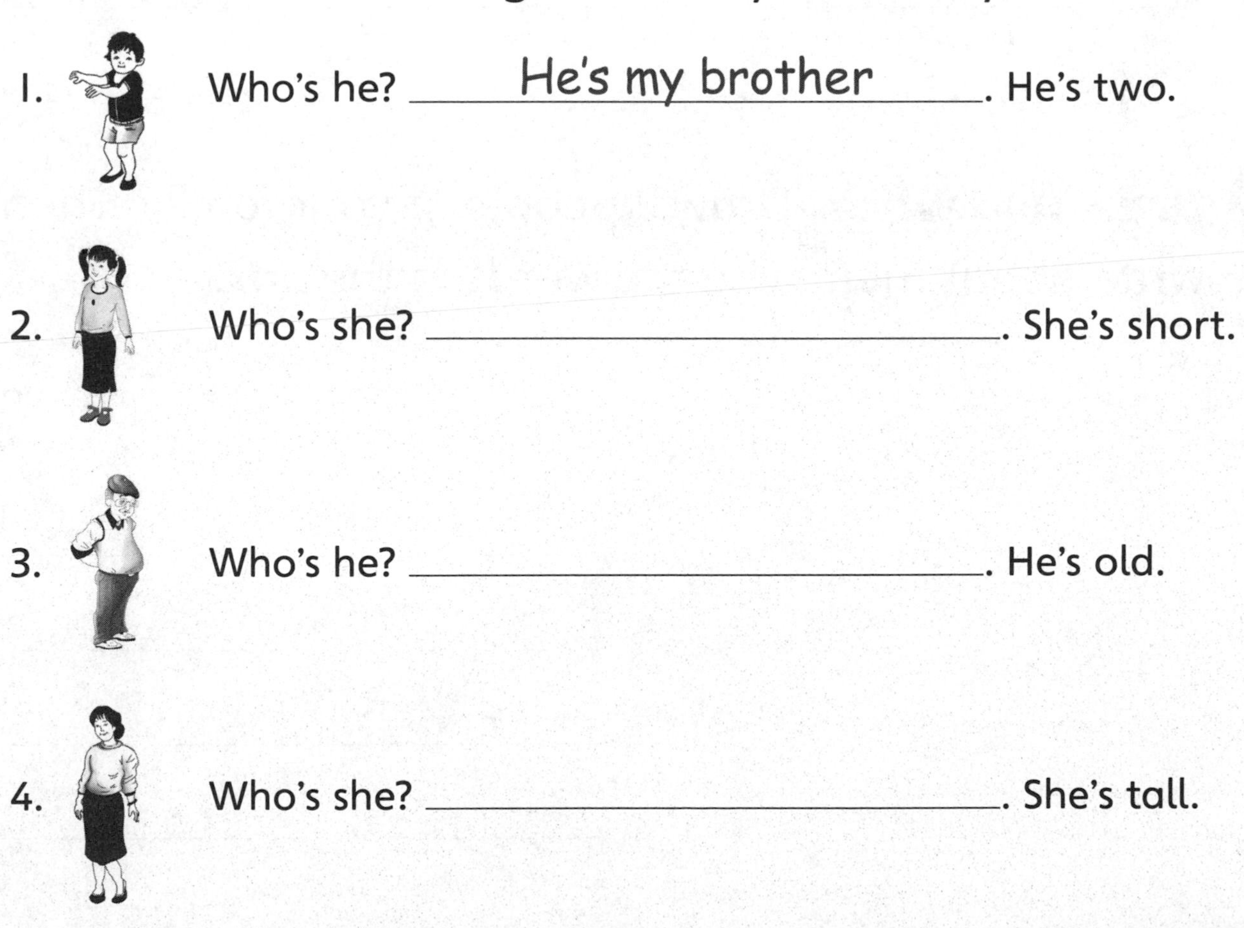

1. Who's he? He's my brother. He's two.
2. Who's she? ____________. She's short.
3. Who's he? ____________. He's old.
4. Who's she? ____________. She's tall.

3 **Write.** Write questions and answers.

1. Who's he ____________________?

He's my big brother. He's tall ____________________. (tall)

2. ____________________?

____________________. (young)

3. ____________________?

____________________. (ten)

4. ____________________?

____________________. (small)

4 **Draw and write.** Draw 2 people in your family. Then write about them. Use the words in the box.

old	short	tall	young

____

____

____

____

Unit 4

Yes/No* questions with *Is there . . . ?

Question			Answer	
Is there	a lamp	in the bedroom?	Yes, **there is.**	*isn't = is not*
	a sofa	in the kitchen?	No, **there isn't.**	

***Is there** a mirror in the kitchen? No, **there isn't**.*

1 **Read.** Look at your house. Circle the letter.

1. Is there a sofa in the bedroom?

   a. Yes, there is. b. No, there isn't.

2. Is there a clock in the kitchen?

   a. Yes, there is. b. No, there isn't.

3. Is there a chair in the living room?

   a. Yes, there is. b. No, there isn't.

4. Is there a lamp in the dining room?

   a. Yes, there is. b. No, there isn't.

2 **Look and write.**

1. Is there a sofa in the bedroom? No, there isn't.

2. ________ a lamp in the bedroom? ________.

3. ________ a clock in the bedroom? ________.

4. ________ a chair in the bedroom? ________.

3 **Look.** Write questions.

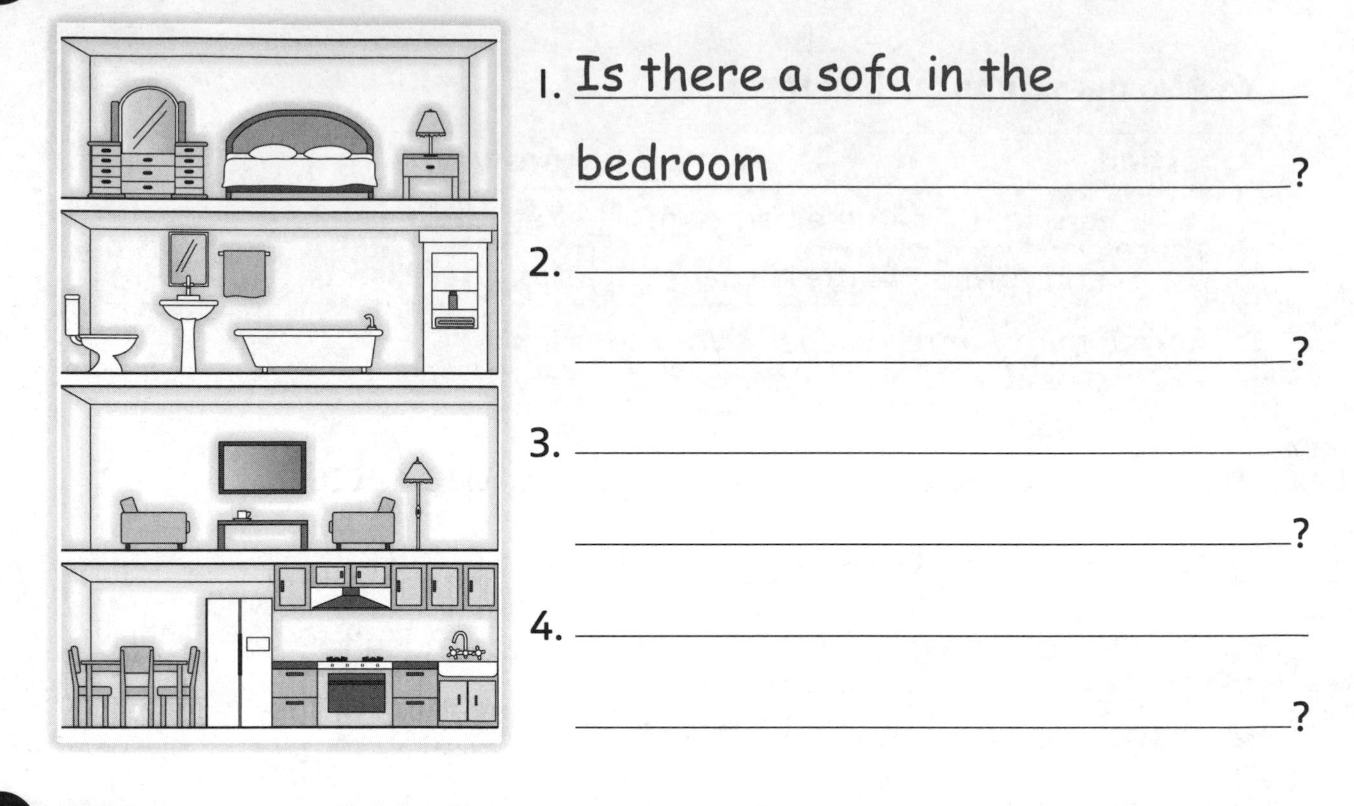

1. Is there a sofa in the bedroom?
2. ____________________?
3. ____________________?
4. ____________________?

4 **Write.** Answer your questions from Activity 3.

1. No, there isn't.
2. ____________________.
3. ____________________.
4. ____________________.

5 **Draw and write.** Draw your living room. Write 2 questions and answers.

Present progressive: *He/She is* + verb-*ing*

Question	Answer
Where is your sister?	She's in the kitchen.

Question			Answer		
What's	she	**doing**?	She's	**eating**.	*What's = What is* *She's = She is*

do → doing   *eat → eating*

1 Look and read. Circle the word.

1.  **She / She's** eating.

3.  **He's / He** taking a bath.

2.  She's **sleeping / sleep**.

4.  He's **watching / watch** TV.

2 Write. Rewrite the sentences. Use *'s*.

1. He is drawing. He's drawing ______________________.
2. She is singing. ______________________.
3. The baby is sleeping in the bedroom. ______________________ ______________________.
4. My brother is watching TV in the living room. ______________________ ______________________.

3 Look and write.

1. Where's your sister?
   She's in the bedroom.
   She's sleeping.

2. ______ your mother?
   ______.
   ______.

3. ______ your brother?
   ______.
   ______.

4. ______ your big sister?
   ______.
   ______.

4 Draw and write. Draw 2 family members at home. Write.

My father's in the kitchen.
He's cooking.
______
______
______
______
______
______

Unit 5

Present progressive: ***am/are/is*** **+ verb-*ing***

<table>
<tr><th colspan="4">Question</th><th colspan="3">Answer</th><th></th></tr>
<tr><td rowspan="3">What</td><td>are</td><td>you</td><td rowspan="3">wearing?</td><td>I’m</td><td rowspan="3">wearing</td><td>white shoes.</td><td rowspan="3">I’m = I am
He’s = He is
She’s = She is</td></tr>
<tr><td rowspan="2">is</td><td>your brother</td><td>He’s</td><td rowspan="2">a hat.</td></tr>
<tr><td>the girl</td><td>She’s</td></tr>
</table>

You can also say:

*My mother**’s wearing** a hat. = My mother **is wearing** a hat.*

*The baby**’s wearing** a hat. = The baby **is wearing** a hat.*

1 Read. Circle.

1. What **is / are** she wearing?
2. What **is / are** you wearing?
3. **She’s / She** wearing a red dress.
4. I **’m / ’re** wearing gloves.
5. You **’s / ’re** wearing socks.
6. I’m **wear / wearing** a skirt.

2 Write. Complete the questions on p. 18.

1. What is your mother wearing?
2. What ________ your brother ________?
3. What ________ your father ________?
4. What ________ you ________?

3 Color and write. Use Activity 2.

1. She's wearing green pants.
2. ________.
3. ________.
4. ________.

4 Look and write.

1. 
What is he wearing?
He's wearing pants.
He's wearing a shirt.

2. 

____

3. 
____

4. 
____

Questions with *that* and *those*

Question		Answer		
What's	**that**?	**That**'s	my pink hat.	*What's = What is*
What are	**those**?	**Those** are	my brown pants.	*That's = That is*

that = one thing

those = two or more things/plurals

1 Look and read. Circle the words. Then match.

1. What's **that** / **those**?
2. What are **that** / **those**?
3. What **'s** / **are** that?
4. What **is** / **are** those?
5. **What's** / **What are** that?

a. **That** / **Those** are my gloves.
b. **That's** / **Those** my hat.
c. **That's** / **Those** my skirt.
d. **That's** / **Those are** my socks.
e. That **'s** / **are** my shirt.

2 Write.

1. What's that ? That's my blue dress.
2. ______________________? Those are my red gloves.
3. ______________________? Those are my black shoes.
4. ______________________? That's my white shirt.
5. ______________________? Those are my brown pants.

3 **Look and write.** Ask and answer questions.

1. What's that ? That's my jacket.
2. ________? ________.
3. ________? ________.
4. ________? ________.

4 **Draw and write.** Draw and color a picture of your clothes. Choose 3 things. Write sentences.

Unit 6

Simple present of *want*: *I/you/he, she*

<table>
<tr><th colspan="4">Question</th><th>Answer</th><th></th></tr>
<tr><td rowspan="2">Do</td><td rowspan="2">you</td><td rowspan="4">want</td><td rowspan="4">a bike?</td><td>Yes, I do.</td><td rowspan="4">don't = do not
doesn't = does not</td></tr>
<tr><td>No, I don't. I want a train.</td></tr>
<tr><td rowspan="2">Does</td><td rowspan="2">he/she</td><td>Yes, he does.</td></tr>
<tr><td>No, she doesn't.
She wants a train.</td></tr>
</table>

To ask a question: ***Do*** *you + want . . . ?* or ***Does*** *he/she + want . . . ?*

Read. Circle the words.

1. **Do / Does** you want a top? Yes, I **do / does**.
2. **Do / Does** he want a train? Yes, he **do / does**.
3. **Do / Does** she want a bike? Yes, she **does / doesn't**.
4. Do you **want / wants** a ball? No, I **don't / do**.

Read and write.

1. Does she want a kite?
2. ________ you want a truck?
3. He ________ a ball.
4. Does your brother ________ a top?
5. Do you ________ a train?
6. I ________ a bike.

3 **Read and write.** Answer the questions.

1. Do you want a game? ______________________________.
2. Do you want a big car? ______________________________.
3. Do you want a sister? ______________________________.
4. Do you want a bike? ______________________________.

4 **Look and write.**

1. she / ☹ — Does she want a train? No, she doesn't.
2. he / ☺ — ______________________________? ______________________________.
3. he / ☹ — ______________________________? ______________________________.
4. she / ☺ — ______________________________? ______________________________.

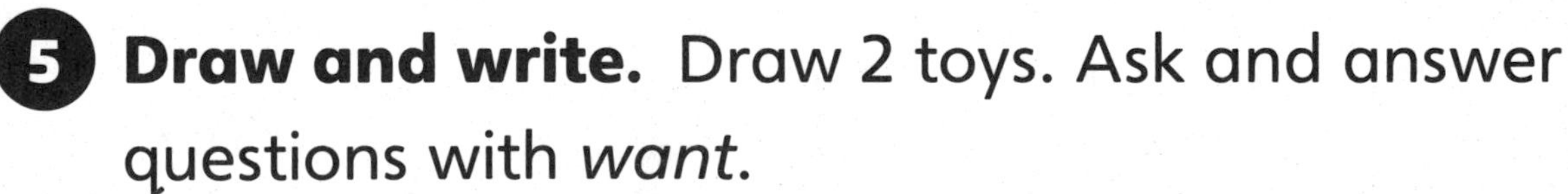

5 **Draw and write.** Draw 2 toys. Ask and answer questions with *want*.

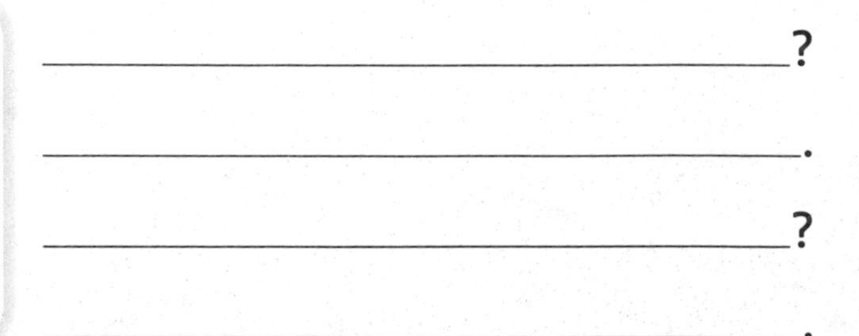

______________________________?

______________________________.

______________________________?

______________________________.

Questions with *this* and *these*

Question		Answer	
Is **this**	your puzzle?	Yes, **it** is.	*isn't = is not*
		No, **it** isn't. **It's** Marco's puzzle.	*It's = It is*
Are **these**	your dolls?	Yes, **they** are.	*aren't = are not*
		No, **they** aren't. **They're** Anita's dolls.	*They're = They are*

For one thing:
*Is **this** your robot? Yes, **it** is.*

For two or more things:
*Are **these** your cars? No, **they** aren't.*

1 Read. Circle the words.

1. Is **this / these** your top?
   No, it **isn't / aren't**.
   It's / They're Juan's top.

2. Are these her **toy / toys**?
   No, they **aren't / isn't**.
   They're / It's my toys.

3. Are **this / these** your balls?
   Yes, **it / they** are.

4. **Are / Is** this your doll?
   No, **it / they** isn't.
   It's her **doll / dolls**.

2 Read and write. Complete the sentences.

1. ____________ your robot?
   Yes, it ____________.

2. ____________ your puzzles?
   No, they ____________. ____________ Bob's puzzles.

3. ____________ her teddy bear?
   No, it ____________.

3 **Look and write.** Ask questions. Follow the model.

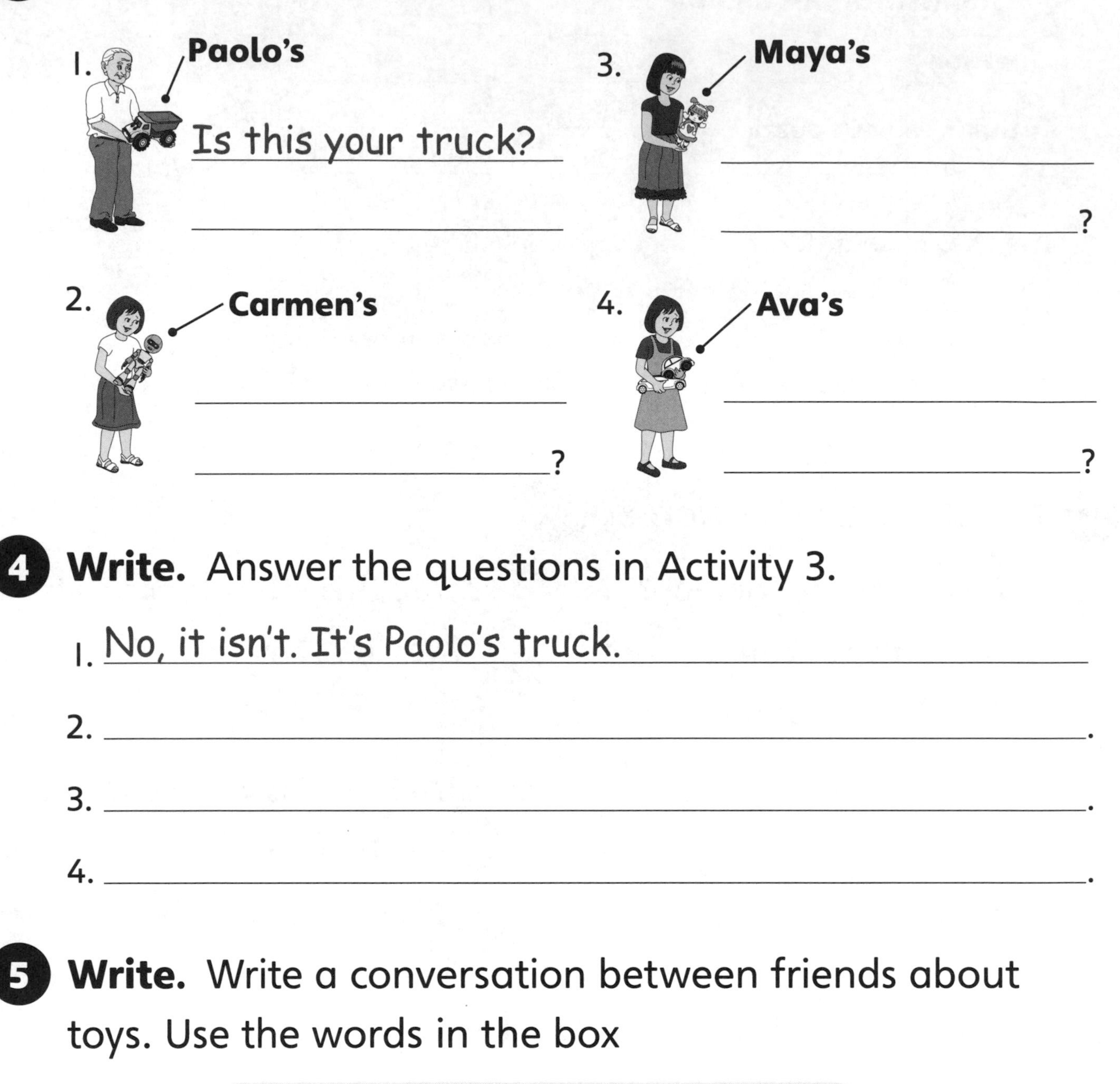

4 **Write.** Answer the questions in Activity 3.

1. No, it isn't. It's Paolo's truck.
2. ______________________.
3. ______________________.
4. ______________________.

5 **Write.** Write a conversation between friends about toys. Use the words in the box

aren't	isn't	these	this

____

____

____

____

Unit 7

Possessive adjectives

I	have	black	hair.	**My**	hair	is	black.
You				**Your**			
He	has			**His**			
She				**Her**			

The sentences have the same meaning:

I have blue eyes. = ***My*** *eyes are blue.*

1 **Look and read.** Circle the word.

1. **His / Your** hair is black.
2. **His / Their** hair is black.
3. **Her / Their** hair is black.
4. **My / Our** hair is black.

   Your / My eyes are black, too!
5. This is my family.

   Our / Your hair is black.

2 **Read and write.** Use the words.

1. hair / short Her hair is short.

   eyes / black ______________________.
2. hair / short ______________________.
3. hair / black ______________________.

   eyes / black / too ______________________

   ______________________.

3 **Read.** Rewrite the sentences.

1. I have short hair. My hair is short ______.
2. My father has big ears. ______.
3. You have small hands. ______.
4. My grandmother and grandfather have white hair.

   ______.
5. My little sister has short legs. ______.
6. My baby brother has a small mouth. ______.

4 **Look and write.** Use *her*, *his*, *my*, and *your*.

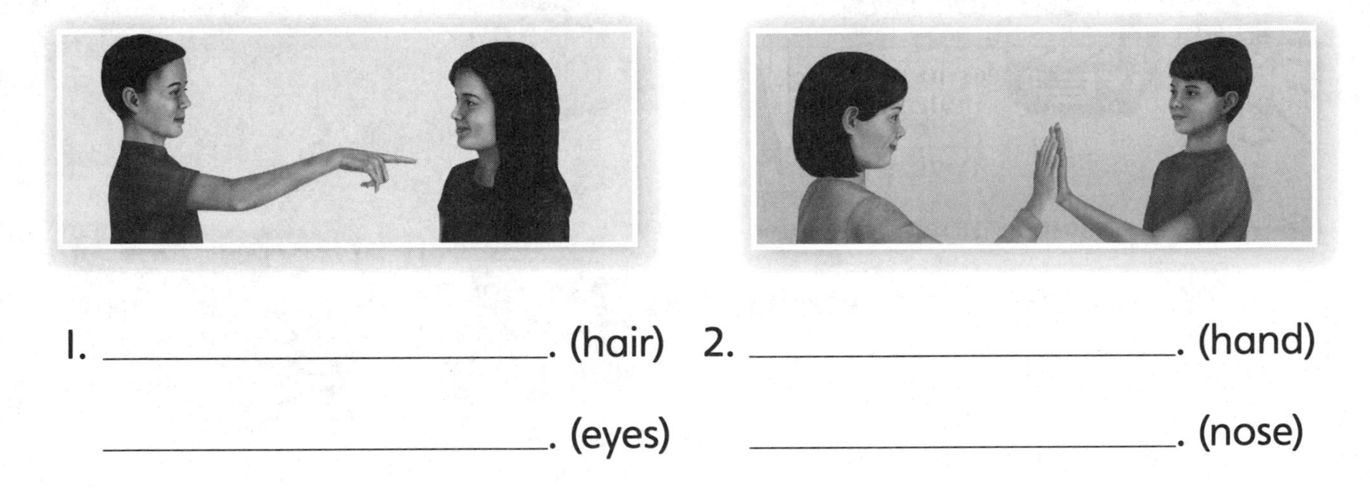

1. ______. (hair) ______. (eyes)
2. ______. (hand) ______. (nose)

5 **Write.** Find a photo of friends or family members. Put it here. Write 4 sentences about it.

Put photo here.

______

______

______

______

______

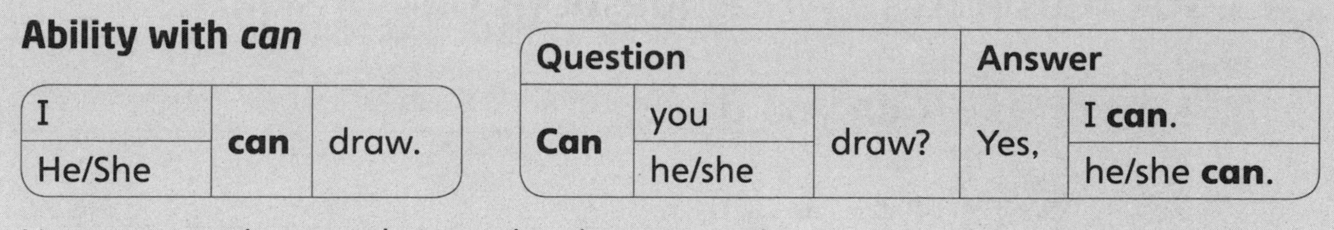

Ability with *can*

I	**can**	draw.
He/She		

Question			Answer	
Can	you	draw?	Yes,	I **can**.
	he/she			he/she **can**.

Use *can* + action word: *I/you/he/she* **can** cook.

1 **Read and match.** Draw a line.

1. I can walk on my hands.
2. I can jump on one foot.
3. She can run and jump.
4. He can walk on his hands, too.

a. He has strong arms.
b. She has strong legs.
c. I have strong arms.
d. I have strong legs.

2 **Write.** Unscramble the words.

1. I / jump / can ________________________________.
2. she / clean / can ________________________________.
3. watch / he / can / TV ________________________________.
4. big / can / my / sister / eat ________________________________.
5. run / you / can ________________________________?

3 **Look and write.** Write 3 sentences. Use *can*.

She can jump.

____

____

____

4 **Look and write.** Write questions and answers.

1. Can you draw ____________________?
   Yes, I can ____________________.
2. ____________________?
   ____________________.
3. ____________________?
   ____________________.
4. ____________________?
   ____________________.

Write. Write 4 sentences about your friends or family. Use *can*.

My father can cook.

____

____

____

____

____

Unit 8

like with count and noncount nouns

Question				Answer	
Do	you	**like**	eggs?	Yes, I **do**.	*don't =* *do not*
				No, I **don't**.	
Does	he		soup?	Yes, he **does**.	*doesn't =* *does not*
				No, he **doesn't**.	

With *like*, say: *I* ***like*** *apples / bananas / eggs*. (Not: ~~*I like apple/banana/egg*~~.)
I ***like*** *soup*. (Not: ~~*I like soups*~~.)

Read. Circle your answer.

1. Do you like fish?
   a. Yes, I do. b. No, I don't.
2. Do you like apples?
   a. Yes, I do. b. No, I don't.
3. Do you like chicken?
   a. Yes, I do. b. No, I don't.
4. Do you like rice?
   a. Yes, I do. b. No, I don't.

2 Read. Write your answer.

1. Do you like computers? ______________________.
2. Do you like kites? ______________________.
3. Do you like robots? ______________________.
4. Do you like puzzles? ______________________.

3 Read and write.

1. Does he like sandwiches? No, he doesn't. He doesn't like sandwiches.
2. ________ you like oranges? Yes, I ________. I like oranges.
3. Does she ________ cookies? Yes, she does. She ________ cookies.
4. Do you ________ soup? No, I don't. I ________ like soup.
5. ________ she ________ eggs? No, she ________ like eggs.

4 **Read.** Write answers that are true for you.

1. Do you want a cookie? No, I don't. I don't like cookies.
2. Do you want some chicken? ________
3. Do you want an apple? ________
4. Do you want some rice? ________

5 **Look and write.** Write about people in your family.

1. 

grandfather Does your grandfather like eggs?

No, he doesn't. He likes chicken.

2. 

mother ________

____

3. 

brother/sister ________

____

4. grandmother ________

____

Indefinite articles: *a, an*

a + consonant	banana, cookie, sandwich
an + vowel (a, e, i, o, u)	arm, eraser, orange

Use *a* or *an* with one thing: ***a*** *banana*, ***a*** *sandwich*, ***an*** *eraser*, ***an*** *orange*.

Don't use *a/an* with these words: *cheese*, *rice*, *soup*, *tea*, *water*, *milk*, *juice*.

1 **Write.** Make 2 lists.

~~apple~~	arm
banana	computer
ear	egg
eraser	fish
mouth	tree

a	an
	apple

Read. Write *a* or *an*.

1. Is it _____ pencil? No, it isn't. It's _____ table.
2. Is it _____ eraser? Yes, it is!
3. Is there _____ sofa in the living room? No, but there's _____ chair.
4. Does he want _____ apple? No. He wants _____ cookie.
5. There's _____ yellow butterfly. It's not _____ orange butterfly.

3 **Look and write.** Complete the sentences.

1. There is a __girl__, an ________, a ________, and an ________.
2. There isn't an ________, a ________, a ________, and an ________.

Look and write.

1. a cookie ______
2. ______
3. ______
4. ______
5. ______
6. ______
7. ______
8. ______

5 **Write.** Complete the sentences. Use all of the words.

~~map~~	chair	egg	eraser
old toy	~~apple~~	sofa	jacket

1. In my classroom, there isn't an apple.
There is a map.
2. In my living room, there ______
______
3. In my kitchen, there ______
______
4. In my bedroom, there ______
______